ZAY  BOY

AND ADVENTURES WITH JESUS

(SHIELD OF FAITH)

ZAYBOY – ROBERT GOINS

Copyright © 2021

First Edition, First Printing
Printed in the United States of America

ISBN - 979-8-8692-6336-0 (Paperback)
ISBN - 979-8-8692-6337-7 (E-book)

Editor: Diana Goins

Author Contact Information:
Robert Goins
http://rgoinsbooks.wix.com
Email: rgoinsbooks@gmail.com

SALVATION
RIGHTEOUSNESS
TRUTH
FAITH
THE SPIRIT
(THE WORD OF GOD)
GOSPEL OF
PEACE

Zay was sitting in the front room reading his bible lesson with his mom. They were reading Ephesians 6. He was captivated by it and wondered how the armor of God would look on him.

"Mom how do you put on the armor of God? And what does it look like?"
"Well, I believe in the Spirit everyone has a glorious suit of armor." She answered.

"Every day you put it on. You have the Belt of Truth. Which means being honest. And the breastplate of righteousness to guard your heart and it helps you do good. And the gospel shoes on your feet to be at peace even when it seems uncomfortable."

"Above all the protective shield of faith to keep you safe from the enemies' attacks. And the helmet of salvation to protect your thoughts, and the sword of the Spirit, which is the Word of God that is the Bible."

I AM THE
FUTURE

"And also, with prayer and petition to keep you alert." Said mom.

"Which one do you use first?"

"You will know by the task at hand."

I AM THE
FUTURE

"Remember to stand in truth, honesty, peace, faith, prayer, and keep the Word in your heart; then you will always be ready."

"I think I can do that. I am a superhero you know."

"Yes, I know. And I am sure you will. Now get your shoes on so we can go visit your sister and nephews. I know you have been waiting."
"Yes!" Zay jumps up to put his shoes on. He loves to visit his older siblings, but especially his nephews.

At his sister's home Zay was playing with his nephews Mari and Davie.

"Are you afraid of the dark?" Mari asked Zay.

"No, I am a superhero, and I am not afraid of the dark."

"You're not a superhero? I know what a superhero looks like and you're not a superhero!"
"Yes, I am a superhero for Jesus! And you can be one too!"

"No, I can't, because I'm afraid of the dark."

"Then we will have to use my superpower to help you not be afraid."
"You have a superpower? What is it?" Mari asked curiously.

"It is the name of Jesus!! When I used it, I defeated my fear of the dark!"

"Jesus lives at church, and we go to His house every Sunday." Said Mari.

"Jesus, lives in our hearts and He gives us faith to be superheroes." Zay puts his hand over his heart.

"Jesus will help me not be afraid?"
"He sure will you just open your
heart and believe that He will, ok?"

"Zay, we will be leaving in 30 minutes!" Mom yells.
"Ok!" Let's play a game before I have to go."
"Ok. What about a superhero game to save Davie from the pamper snatcher?"
"Awesome, we will save you Davie!"

After returning home Zay was in constant prayer for Mari not to be afraid of the dark. So that night, as he continued to pray, he found himself in Mari's room.

Mari was wide awake and afraid.
"It's ok Mari I am here! I'm Zay boy!"
"I'm scared. Do you hear that noise?"

I AM THE

"I hear it, but Jesus is with us, and His name is my superpower." "Leave Mari alone in the name of Jesus!" Zay Shouted. But the noise continued.

I AM THE
FUTURE

"I don't understand. I used the name." Zay thought.
Jesus explains, "Mari is afraid. Use your faith to shield him from the sound of fear first, and then use my name."

"My faith?" Zay recalled the shield of faith. He also remembered that the Spirit of fear is not from God, and thought on the memory verse he had learned from kid's church.

I AM THE
TURE

2 Timothy 1:7 For God has not given us a spirit of fear, but of power and of love and of a sound mind.

Soon Zay had a shield on his arm.

He lifted the shield up over Mari to block the sound. Now he could only hear the comforting words of Jesus.

"It is ok Mari. I am with you always." Said Jesus.

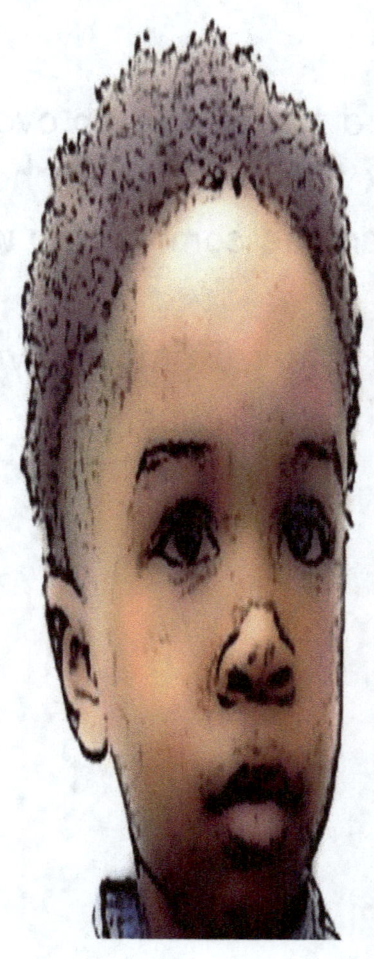

"Yes, I have Jesus with me!"
Shouted Mari.
The Spirit of fear had nothing to
draw strength from, because of
the peace of Jesus, Mari wasn't
scared any more.

"I command you to leave now in the name of Jesus. We are not afraid." Zay said, then the sound stopped.

"That was awesome. Am I a superhero too now?" Mari asked. "You can be. I need more brave superheroes like you too." Jesus said.

Zay ended up back in his room and could not wait to see Mari on their next visit. "What an adventure and now I have a shield!"

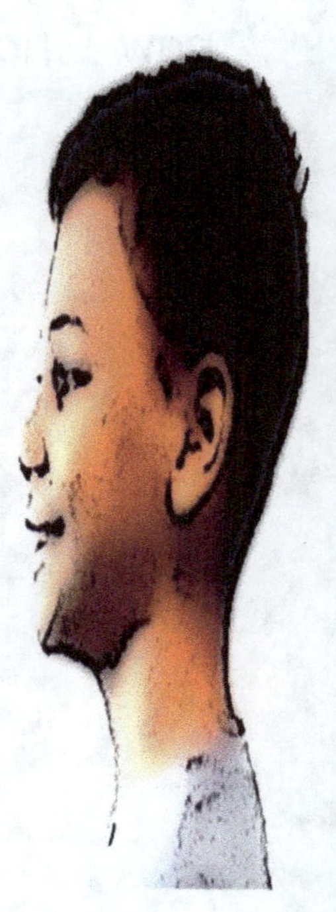

The next visit had come, and Mari was excited to talk to Zay about what had happened.
"I'm not afraid anymore!!" Mari said.

"I am a superhero like you!"
"I know and now you need a name!"
"I have one! I am Super Mario Kid!"
Said Mari.

"No, not that name. We have to think of one cooler." Said Zay.
"What about, Fearless Boy?"
"I like fearless boy, because I am not scared anymore."

Zay-Boy was happy that he could help. But begins to ponder how he will gather each piece of the armor needed to fulfill the rest of his superhero purpose and who else will become a superhero along the way....

TO BE CONTINUED...

There are more
adventures to come.

Do You want to be a Superhero for Jesus?

Continue to follow Zayboy and find out how!!

SMALL BUT
NOTICED!!!

ARE YOU READY!!

LET'S GO, ON AN ADVENTURE!!!